W9-AAE-587

God's Gift

God's Gift

Over 100 Studs, Stallions and Dreamboats from the 70s and 80s

First published in 2006 by
Michael O'Mara Books Limited
9 Lion Yard
Tremadoc Road
London SW4 7NQ

Copyright © Michael O'Mara Books Ltd 2006

All rights reserved. No part of this publication may be reproduced,
stored in a retrieval system, or transmitted by any means, without the
prior permission in writing of the publisher, nor be otherwise circulated
in any form of binding or cover other than that in which it is published
and without a similar condition including this condition being imposed
on the subsequent purchaser.

A CIP catalogue record for this book is available from the British Library.

ISBN (10 digit): 1-84317-214-3
ISBN (13 digit): 978-1-84317-214-7

1 3 5 7 9 10 8 6 4 2

Designed by www.envydesign.co.uk

Printed and bound in Italy by L.E.G.O.

www.mombooks.com

Acknowledgements

A GREAT MANY people have been involved in the making of this book. The editors would like to thank the whole team at Michael O'Mara Books, especially Jane Carson, for the original ideas and brainstorming sessions. Thanks also to Miranda Sheath and Claire Banyard for their contribution to the *God's Gift* wish list; and to Lindsay Davies, Matt Foss, Kate Gribble, Louise Hall, Tanveer Minhas, Duncan Moore, Hannah Robinson, Ana Sampson, Ruth Shippobotham and Tim Stapleton for the captions. Lucie Cave provided the fabulous Foreword, while Envy Design have excelled with the design of both the cover and insides.

Finally, sincere thanks to Judith Palmer, picture researcher extraordinaire, who had the enviable task of spending hours tracking down the sexiest, funniest, hunkiest pictures of the studs, stallions and dreamboats who fill these pages. It was a tough job, but someone had to do it.

Foreword

YOU NEVER FORGET your first love. And I'm not talking about the spotty compatriots of your youth, or even that dangerous older boy who – shock, horror! – smoked cigarettes *on school grounds*. Instead, think back to the time when your favourite pin-ups ruled your world – when your bedroom was plastered floor to ceiling with technicoloured talent; pencil cases and school books were smothered in stickers bearing your beloved's image; and nights were spent imagining yourself as Mrs Jason Donovan, or Mrs Richard Gere, or Mrs Sean Connery … (decisions, decisions). Ah, those were the days. Back then, we all had our very own perfect pseudo-boyfriends – heroes who would never let us down, pull our hair or shriek 'Girls smell!' Those guys really had it all: fabulous physiques, come-to-bed eyes, macho charisma yet soulful sensitivity … and of course in our lovestruck imaginations they had eyes only for us. No wonder they stole our hearts. Forget, for the moment, the dodgy fashion sense and the questionable poses: remember instead the blissful hours of stargazing and daydreaming that these pin-ups afforded us.

Yes, for every girl (or guy) who has worshipped at the altar of Adonis, this is a chance to revisit those glorious years when a whole afternoon could be spent in devoted contemplation of a single, slightly dog-eared, Morten Harket poster. Taking a mouthwatering meander through the pin-ups of the past, *God's Gift* catalogues the cutest smiles, whitest teeth and cheesiest poses ever to be caught on camera. Inside these pages, over 100 hot hunks await your discerning eye, their good looks and bronzed bodies crying out to be ogled. If you have ever gazed wistfully at a pair of gleaming pecs, or yearned to trail your fingers over the corrugated contours of a washboard stomach, this is the book for you.

All the tools, the attributes, the accessories of male seductive charm are here, and in all their understated glory: the long, lithe limbs; the toned, tanned torso; the impossibly dense mane of hair (or, for the less hirsutely gifted, the carefully polished pate); the teasing, come-hither glance; the dazzling, predatory smile; the glitzy medallion; the tight, cheese-cutter jeans; the navel-skimming Hawaiian shirt; the saucy Stetson … From the Brat Pack to the Bee Gees, David Cassidy to David Hasselhoff, Adam Ant to Duran Duran, *God's Gift* lays on a feast for all, with totty to tempt every tastebud. Do studmuffins from the seventies float your boat? Or was it the heartthrobs of the eighties that set your pulse racing and your temperature rising? Be it country-and-western cowboys, butch bikers, silver-screen sex bombs or raunchy warblers that take your breath away, *God's Gift* delivers on every front (and, in the case of racing driver James Hunt, very nearly full frontal).

Of course, dreamy though these gentlemen are, we ladies are no longer the star-struck, (not so) bright young things we once were. We now have jobs, handbags, breasts, and all the other grown-up paraphernalia maturity brings. And – erm, how shall I put this? – in some cases our tastes have moved on too. While a fleet of dreamboats are still seaworthy, with snapshots showing them to be fully rigged and ready even after all these years, others aren't quite so, well, shipshape. Be it fashion fiascos, hairdo horrors or a simple case of 'What *were* they thinking?', *God's Gift* is not afraid to include the pics that some stars might prefer us *not* to revisit: early shots of modern-day marvels (eat your heart out, Brad Pitt); a potpourri of peculiar poses (and poseurs); cheesy chaps who really put the *fromage* into a photo shoot; and rock stars who are open for ridicule. Gaze and wonder why we (and they) ever thought they looked hot, hot, hot – while secretly thinking that there's just something about a mullet on a man …

Call it nostalgia, call it lechery, call it the ideal way to spend an afternoon – there's no doubting that *God's Gift* is utterly irresistible. Crowded with snaps of the guys who once made us weak at the knees, every page is a homage to the hunk, a celebration of the sex symbol, a tribute to testosterone that will keep you up all night. Relish the reunion with singers who made us swoon, actors who made us ache with longing, and sports stars who made us realize P.E. wasn't all bad. You can keep your groomed and polished Messrs Timberlake, Beckham and Bloom – the real deal's right here: before stylists and airbrushing; before celebs cottoned on to controlling their image; before most of today's stars were even born. Give us love handles, frizz and outrageous costumes. Give us macho men, bodybuilders and lovelorn-looking boys. Give us naked flesh, baby oil and seriously bad-hair days. Forget the man-made … here are the real men.

So switch your phone to automatic voicemail, don't answer the door, and put your out-of-office response on your email. Turn all your attention to the tasty treats to follow. Prepare for a provocative experience that will make you giggle, sigh, smile and reminisce. Let yourself once more fall under the spell of these hairy beefcakes, these seductive señors, these muscle men oozing with sex appeal. Take a retrospective ride through pin-up paradise.

You never forget your first love. This book reminds you – without a shadow of a doubt – just why.

Lucie Cave, 2006

Burt Reynolds outsmouldering his cigar, as usual.

Tom Cruise:
Position Impossible.

Scott Baio seems more chilly than Chachi.

◀ *Engelbert Humperdinck:*
original King of Bling.

*Keep smiling, **Jean-Claude Van Damme** – perhaps no one will notice you've forgotten your weights.*

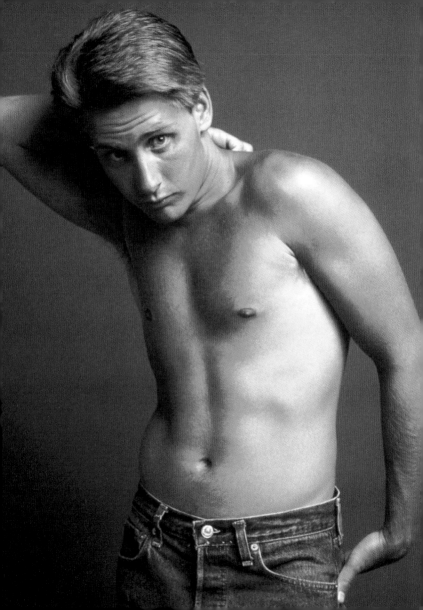

Sylvester Stallone: less Rambo, *more* Pretty in Pink.

◀ *Emilio Estevez worries that his deodorant isn't working.*

The Bee Gees:
foil-wrapped for freshness.

Europe *provide the final countdown for mullets everywhere.*

David Cassidy's mama
always wanted a girl.

13

Dolph Lundgren will do anything to impress the ladies – even grow a pair of red antlers.

15

Denzel Washington works the high-school-yearbook look.

David Hasselhoff: small pants, big pole.

17

Corey Haim: *this lost boy's*
(trying to be) all man.

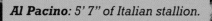

Al Pacino: *5' 7" of Italian stallion.*

◀ **Paul Stanley** *from KISS dresses to the right.*

Mark Spitz *(left)* and ***David Wilkie*** *proudly show off the chocolate money Santa gave them.*

23

Eddie Kidd: famed
for the throbbing beast
between his legs.

Donny Osmond feels like chicken tonight.

◀ **Christian Slater**: lipsmackingly luscious.

*Who wants to be on **Telly** (**Savalas**) tonight?*

*Pity the fool … **Mr T** blings it on.*

*Does anyone fancy a jump off a **Cliff** (**Richard**)?*

*You might be pointing to it, **Andy Gibb**, but we still can't see it.*

Spandau Ballet love
a good wedding.

We won't let you be
lonesome tonight,
Elvis Presley.

◀ **Nick Kamen** – sadly, just before
he put the Levis in for a wash.

Mel Gibson: *hello, sailor.*

Eddie Murphy: ▶
(Beverly Hills) Cop a load of this!

Andrew McCarthy:
pretty in pastel.

Starsky and Hutch: *crime capers in casual knitwear.*

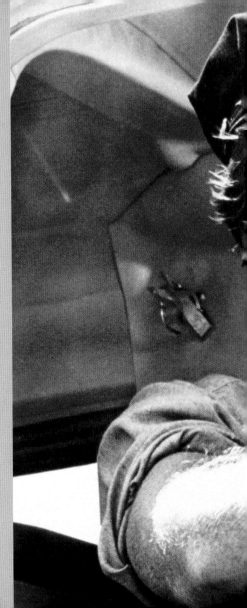

*One look from **Robert Redford** jams all the ladies' frequencies.*

FREQUENCY
JAMMER

*Nobody puts (**Patrick**) **Swayze** in the corner.*

◀ **Kevin Costner**: *I will always love me.*

Warren Beatty: so vain,
he probably thinks this
caption's about him.

◀ *Michel Polnareff* started to think
his wedding outfit was misjudged.

Vanilla Ice: everybody's favourite flavour.

*We go goo-goo over **Limahl**.*

***Miles O'Keeffe:** You Tarzan, ▶ we game for anything …*

Bruce Springsteen: *born with a passion for line-dancing fashion.*

Judd 'Stud'
Nelson.

George: Best before 1980.

*Paul Newman drives ▶
us wild in the west.*

Oliver Tobias:
The Stud. Need
we say more?

◀ *Robert Palmer:*
smell my fingers.

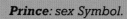

Prince: sex Symbol.

*Michael J. Fox*y

Richard gets ▶
his **Gere** off.

Lou Diamond Phillips *is a girl's best friend.*

Paul Young looks calm,
despite trapping his
fingers in the door.

Morten Harket:
worth taking on.

Tim Robbins: ▶
oven ready.

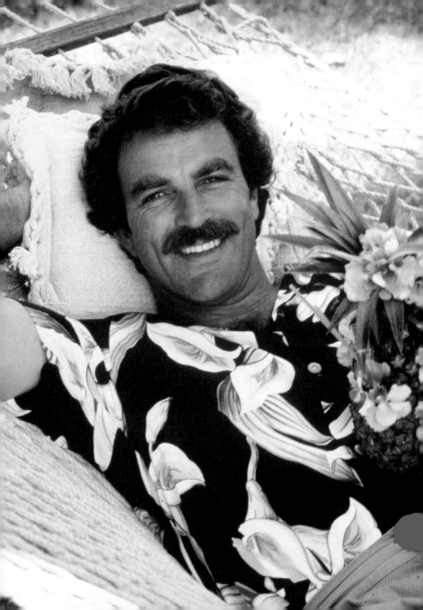

Michael Caine*'s not after
an Italian *job with come-on
eyes like that ...*

◀ ***Tom Selleck****: Anyone fancy
a lick of this Magnum?*

67

Andre Agassi: *game, set and wax?*

Whitesnake's **David Coverdale**: body of an athlete, hair of a dog.

◀ Cheers, **Ted Danson**!

Rick Springfield:
'Mmm ... Feel the quality.'

Gérard Depardieu:
French fancy.

Simon Le Bon:
*you can leave
your socks on.*

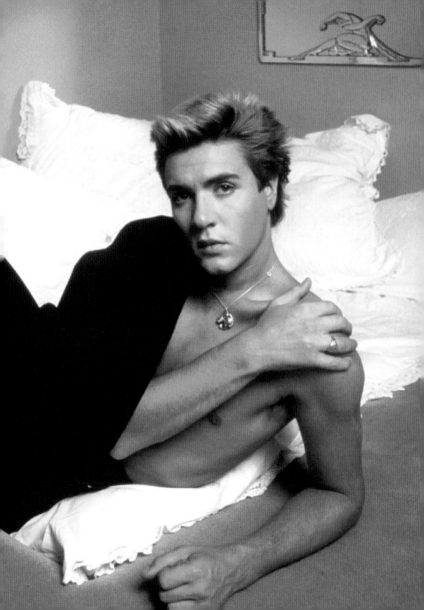

Marc Bolan: *look at the tits on that!*

*Can we help you with ▶
your handcuffs, Officer
(**Steve**) **Guttenberg**?*

C. MAHONEY

Lionel Richie: once, twice, three times a ladies' man.

*Don't tempt Bouncer with your sausage, **Craig McLachlan**.*

Bruce Willis: pose hard with a vengeance.

Barry White: built for comfort, not for speed.

*Is that a microphone in your pants, **Mick Jagger**, or are you just pleased to see us?*

Julio Iglesias: all
teeth and torso.

Matt Dillon:
simply to die for.

Van Halen's
David Lee Roth:
small trousers,
big hair.

*It wasn't just the length of **Tom Hanks's** stem that impressed the ladies.*

Tony Blackburn shows off his Lego hair.

*We love a man in ▶ uniform, **Sean Penn**.*

Bryan Ferry: *suave, sophisticated … and somewhat sinister.*

That outfit should
be copacabanned,
Barry Manilow.

Val Kilmer:
the Iceman cometh ...

Jason Donovan:
*the original boy
next door.*

Les McKeown: 'Do you like my golden nugget?'

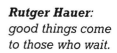

Rutger Hauer:
good things come
to those who wait.

Lee Majors: *six-million-dollar six-pack.*

Errol Brown *from*
Hot Chocolate:
knight in white satin.

Billy Idol
yanks his chain.

Bros: take two into the shower.

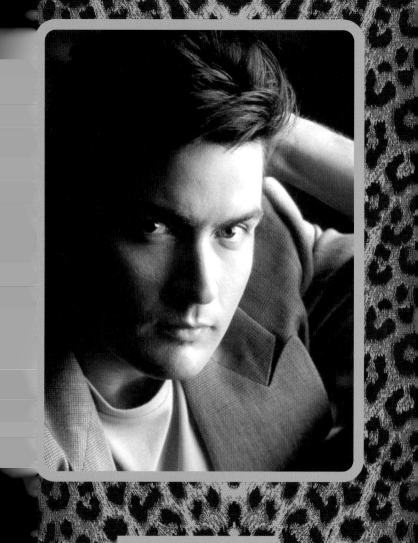

Charlie Sheen: a hot shot by anyone's standards.

John Travolta: bet you look
good on the dance floor.

◀ *Oh Mickey (Rourke),
you're so fine ...*

Erik Estrada *wonders if his seduction technique is looking a little obvious.*

Sean Connery: *double 'oh' heaven.*

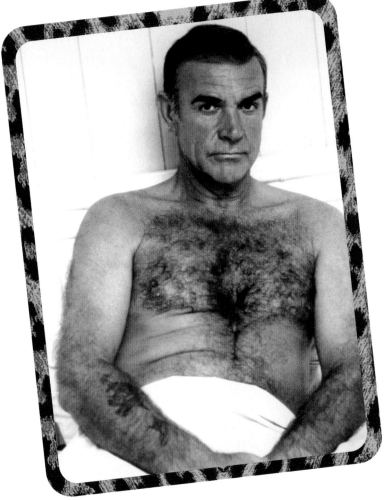

David Bowie: *'Look, no hands!'*

Richard Chamberlain:
Dr Killer Stare.

113

Kurt Russell: *goldie boy.*

Adam Ant: *Prince Charming.*

Duran Duran: *these wild boys are so good they named them twice.*

◀ **James Hunt** just
misses out on showing
us his pole position.

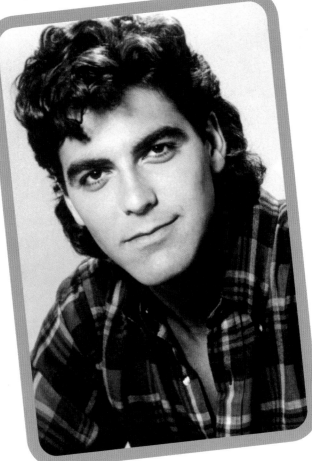

Wham!: *The teeth are ▶ bright, the skin is orange.*

'Maggie, may I borrow your clothes?' asks **Rod Stewart**.

Neil Diamond wishes he'd used Head & Shoulders.

Roger Moore – *with a name like that, he was guaranteed a place in the God's Gift* Hall *of Fame.*

Matthew Broderick: ▶
the cable-knit guy.

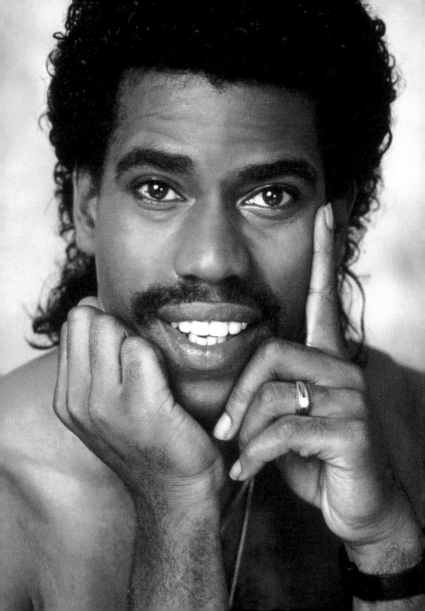

Does Daisy know you've been using
her hair products, **John Schneider**?

Patrick Duffy: Ewing – y'would. ▶

Michael Hutchence: *hair in excess.*

Harrison Ford doesn't
have to go solo.

We'd help **Kris Kristofferson**
make it through the night any day.

Pierce Brosnan knows how to Remington Steele our hearts.

◀ *Jon Bon Jovi*: Wanted – dead or alive.

David: the man who puts the 'sex' into '**Essex**'.

◀ *Nit nurses were much sexier in those days,*
weren't they, ***Arnold Schwarzenegger***?

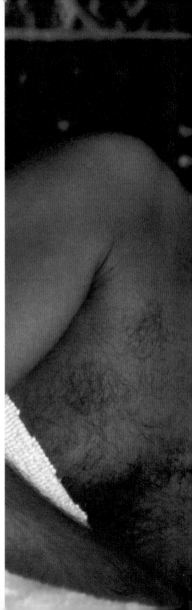

Tom Jones*:*
boyo, oh boyo!

Picture Credits

p. 1 Sipa Press / Rex Features
p. 2-3 SNAP / Rex Features
p. 4 S. Garritano / Rex Features
p. 5 Shooting Star / Idols Licensing and Publicity Limited
p. 6-7 © Patrick Roberts / Sygma / Corbis
p. 8 Shooting Star / Idols Licensing and Publicity Limited
p. 9 Kip Rano / Rex Features
p. 10-11 Everett Collection / Rex Features
p. 12 © Lynn Goldsmith / Corbis
p. 13 ABC / The Kobal Collection
p. 14-15 © Roger Ressmeyer / Corbis
p. 16 Harry Langdon / Shooting Star / Idols Licensing and Publicity Limited
p. 17 Everett Collection / Rex Features
p. 18 The Kobal Collection
p. 19 SNAP / Rex Features
p. 20 © Lynn Goldsmith / Corbis
p. 21 © Douglas Kirkland / Corbis
p. 22 Everett Collection / Rex Features
p. 23 Steve Lewis / Rex Features
p. 24-5 George Richardson / Rex Features
p. 26 Shooting Star / Idols Licensing and Publicity Limited
p. 27 Everett Collection / Rex Features
p. 28 Henry Diltz / Corbis
p. 29 Sipa Press / Rex Features
p. 30 © Gered Mankowitz / Redferns
p. 31 © Lynn Goldsmith / Corbis
p. 32-3 © Michael Putland / RetnaUK
p. 34 Andre Csillag / Rex Features
p. 35 Everett Collection / Rex Features
p. 36 SNAP / Rex Features
p. 37 John Dee / Rex Features
p. 38 The Kobal Collection
p. 39 Rex Features
p. 40-1 SNAP / Rex Features
p. 42 SNAP / Rex Features
p. 43 © Neal Preston / Corbis
p. 44-5 SNAP / Rex Features
p. 46 © Tony Frank / Sygma / Corbis
p. 47 © S.I.N. / Corbis
p. 48-9 © Neal Preston / Corbis
p. 50 Andre Csillag / Rex Features
p. 51 SNAP / Rex Features
p. 52 © GAB Archives / Redferns
p. 53 Sipa Press / Rex Features
p. 54 © Bettman / Corbis
p. 55 Rex Features
p. 56 Rex Features
p. 57 Richard Young / Rex Features
p. 58-9 © Neal Preston / Corbis
p. 60 Kip Rano / Rex Features
p. 61 SNAP / Rex Features
p. 62 SNAP / Rex Features
p. 63 Rex Features
p. 64 Ilpo Musto / Rex Features
p. 65 SNAP / Rex Features
p. 66 CBS-TV / The Kobal Collection

PICTURE CREDITS

p. 67 SNAP / Rex Features

p. 68-9 Peter Stone / Rex Features

p. 70 Everett Collection / Rex Features

p. 71 Dave Hogan / Hulton Archive / Getty Images

p. 72 © Henry Diltz / Corbis

p. 73 Araldo di Crollalanza / Rex Features

p. 74-5 Andy Rosen / Rex Features

p. 76 © Neal Preston / Corbis

p. 77 SNAP / Rex Features

p. 78-9 Araldo di Crollalanza / Rex Features

p. 80 Brendan Beirne / Rex Features

p. 81 © Walter McBride / Retna Ltd

p. 82 © Patricia Steur / Sunshine / Retna

p. 83 © Lynn Goldsmith / Corbis

p. 84-5 Santi Visalli / Getty Images

p. 86 Robin Platzer / Time Life Pictures / Getty Images

p. 87 Allstar

p. 88 © Lynn Goldsmith / Corbis

p. 89 Deborah Feingold / Getty Images

p. 90 © BBC Photo Library / Redferns

p. 91 Orion / The Kobal Collection

p. 92-3 Terry O'Neill / Hulton Archive / Getty Images

p. 94 Paramount / The Kobal Collection

p. 95 Pictorial Press

p. 96 Adrian Boot / RetnaUK

p. 97 © Fin Costello / Redferns

p. 98-9 Terry O'Neill / Getty Images

p. 100 ABC-TV: The Kobal Collection

p. 101 © Fin Costello / Redferns

p. 102 © Neal Preston / Corbis

p. 103 © GAB Archives / Redferns

p. 104 © Neil Mathews / RetnaUK / Retna Ltd, USA

p. 105 © Sandra Johnson / RetnaUK

p. 106 © Kal Yee / Retna Ltd

p. 107 Universal / The Kobal Collection

p. 108-9 © Shooting Star / Idols Licensing and Publicity Limited

p. 110 Allstar / Cinetext / United Artists

p. 111 Sipa Press / Rex Features

p. 112 Jack Robinson / Hulton Archive / Getty Images

p. 113 Shooting Star / Idols Licensing and Publicity Limited

p. 114 Warner Bros / The Kobal Collection

p. 115 Robert Mathew / RetnaUK / Retna Ltd, USA

p. 116-7 © Michael Putland / RetnaUK

p. 118 John Curtis / Rex Features

p. 119 Globe Photos Inc / Rex Features

p. 120 Shooting Star / Idols Licensing and Publicity Limited

p. 121 © Gered Mankowitz / Redferns

p. 122 © Andy Freeberg / Retna Ltd

p. 123 © RB / Redferns

p. 124 The Kobal Collection

p. 125 © Alen MacWeeney / Corbis

p. 126 Deborah Feingold / Getty Images

p. 127 Allstar

p. 128 Everett Collection / Rex Features

p. 129 CBS Photo Archive / Getty Images

p. 130 © Lynn Goldsmith / Corbis

p. 131 © Michel Linssen / Redferns

p. 132 Sipa Press / Rex Features

p. 133 IPC Magazines: CHAT / Rex Features

p. 134 Lucasfilm / 20th Century Fox / The Kobal Collection

p. 135 Jack Robinson / Hulton Archive / Getty Images

p. 136 Deborah Feingold / Getty Images

p. 137 Globe Photos Inc / Rex Features

p. 138-9 © Hulton-Deutsch Collection / Corbis

p. 140 White Mountain Productions / The Kobal Collection

p. 141 David McGough / DMI / Time Life Pictures / Getty Images

p. 142-3 Terry O'Neill / Getty Images

Index

INDEX

Rourke, Mickey 106
Roussos, Demis 103
Russell, Kurt 114

Savalas, Telly 28
Schneider, John 128
Schwarzenegger,
    Arnold 140
Selleck, Tom 66
Sheen, Charlie 105
Slater, Christian 26
Spandau Ballet 32
Spitz, Mark 22
Springfield, Rick 72
Springsteen, Bruce 52
Stallone, Sylvester 9
Stanley, Paul 20
Starsky and Hutch 39
Stewart, Rod 123
Sutherland, Kiefer 21
Swayze, Patrick 43

T, Mr 29
Tobias, Oliver 57
Travolta, John 107
Tyler, Steven 131

Van Damme,
    Jean-Claude 6
Vanilla Ice 48

Washington, Denzel 17
Wham! 121
White, Barry 82
Wilkie, David 23
Willis, Bruce 81
Winkler, Henry 119

Young, Paul 63